CAPE BRETON ISLAND

Photographs by
Warren Gordon MPA

This page: Sydney Harbour Opposite: Great Bras d'Or Channel Title Page: Ingonish Bay Cover: Neil's Harbour Back Cover: Terre Noire

Photographs: Warren Gordon, except where noted by Katheryn Gordon
Graphic Design: Gordon B. Isnor

Special thanks to my good friend, Sherman Hines

Thanks to Charlotte MacLean, Renata MacDonald. Marjorie MacQueen & Murdock Smith.

PUBLISHED BY
Gordon Photographic Ltd.
367 Charlotte St., Sydney
Nova Scotia, Canada, B1P 1E1.
Tel: (902) 564-5665 • Fax: (902) 562-4517
E-mail: gordonphoto@ns.sympatico.ca • Website: www.gordonphoto.com

ISBN: 0-9690395-5-7

Printed in China -L

This one is dedicated to Cape Bretoners
worldwide who continue to encourage
me and give my books a home.

Warren Gordon

Chedabucto Bay

Port Hawkesbury

Petit-De-Grat   Isle Madame

L'Ardoise

Pt. Michaud Beach

Dundee

Soldiers Cove

St. Mary's Church, Big Pond   Ben Eoin

St. Mary's Church, East Bay

Sydney River

Warren paddles in the backyard, Sydney River. Photograph by Katheryn Gordon.

Sydney Harbour

Sydney Boardwalk

Wentworh Park, Sydney   2nd Battalion Nova Scotia Highlanders, "Cape Breton Highlanders"

Glace Bay Harbour

Gabarus   Fourchu

Fortress Louisbourg

Havenside, Louisbourg

Lighthouse Point, Louisbourg

North Sydney

Point Aconi

Drummond Memorial United Church, Boularderie

Great Bras d'Or Channel

Seal Island Bridge

St. Anns Harbour

St. Anns Harbour

Nova Scotia Gaelic College,
St . Anns.

Barachois River

Ingonish Ferry

Ingonish

Neils Harbour

Dingwall

Aspy Bay   White Point

Bay St. Lawrence

Capstick

Buddhist monastery Gampo Abbey.   Opposite: Pleasant Bay

Presqu'ile Beach

Cheticamp

Grand Etang   St. Joseph Du Moine

St. Joseph Du Moine

Terre Noire

Margaree Harbour

Whale Cove

Margaree

East Margaree

Margaree

Margaree

Margaree

Margaree

Margaree

Margaree

Bucklaw

Little Narrows

St. Andrew's Church, Whycocomagh

Grand Narrows

St. Columba Church, Iona

Kidston Island   Alexander Graham Bell Museum, Baddeck

Baddeck

Lake Ainslie

Lake Ainslie

Inverness Beach

Inverness

Glenora Falls

Mabou Coal Mines

Mabou Beach

Mabou

Port Hood

Creignish